DEALING WITH A NARCISSIST

Understanding a Narcissist, Having excellent knowledge about Narcissists' Techniques, Avoiding a Narcissist, A Relationship With a Narcissist, And How to Help a Narcissist

AUTHOR

BRANDON FILIP, PETER COOPER

TABLE OF CONTENTS

INTRODUCTION

Dealing with a narcissist is threatening! If you've had a personal experience, you'd have no doubt believing this! Some individuals, perhaps even you, are undergoing a sickening relationship where the other party demands that they are showered with extreme attention, and often time, constant praise. But you might wonder, is this demand wrong in themselves? Well, actually, no! But this is where we can fault this demand, instead of treating the other party the way they want to be treated, they don't and will even go into the extreme of placing zero attention to the other party's emotion and thought. This type of relationship can spring up from either your family, friends and even coworkers. No sane person will find this appealing!

Often time, we are met with people that thinks and speaks like they know better than or are better off others, and that thinking prompts them to expect homage and respect. To make it even worse, some are quick to criticize people's opinions, they heap insults just because of an action that seems not correct to them, however, when a slight correction is given to them- in fact, if it is in a kind manner, they flare up and would never welcome any constructive criticism thrown at them.

Sadly, these brief highlights aren't all there is about Narcissism. There is more! But If you can accurately relate with this brief highlight and you've been wrestling this menace, it is high time it stops! Now is the time where you can take control of the situation. Nevertheless, if you've never been treated like that or you aren't sure if you have, you didn't make a wrong choice perching. Though succinct, you will gain deep insight into what Narcissism is. To solidify your conviction, here is the breakdown of what you hope to enjoy.

To start with, the very first section of this book will give full detail about who a narcissist is. And why this is essential is because there seems to be a broad definition for the term, leaving some confused as to what to agree to be a narcissist behavior. Additionally, there have been questions about how narcissists are made. Is it an inherited trait or probably something you can cultivate; can you even develop the habit unintentionally? There is more to narcissism background. These backgrounds are oblivious to many, and regrettably, there are improper conclusion people make leading to weird believe that doesn't relate to what happens in the actual realm of Narcissism. To wrap up the section, there exists a question that bothers many. Which is if Narcissism can be healed or cured. Some felt maybe the only help is guiding against Narcissism, but are not sure if an individual with the trait will be cured of these negative traits; you have to read on to get convincing answers to those questions.

The next section is dedicated to digging more explicit on Narcissism; it will highlight the different types of narcissism. There are three known types of Narcissism, and the harm and impact vary. Some people are exhibitionists narcissist; some are only a covert or closet narcissist, and some are even toxic Narcissist. Understanding the differences will give you an edge on how you can deal with a narcissist. For example, if you know that a person is an exhibitionists narcissist, you will be armed on how to deal with such an individual accurately.

The third section is highly dedicated to providing detailed and core solution to the trauma you may have been fighting a long time ago. And that is how you can avoid any narcissism coming your way. Frankly, at this stage, even though the point is laid bare, you will undoubtedly need to read with optimum concentration. It will first highlight the techniques that are being used and adopted by narcissists; also, today, there are secrets about the ways in which Narcissist manipulate an individual which accurate information on that, you can stop being their bait! You should be able to spot how to halt them from afar and let them be aware of their action - subtly!

Furthermore, have you ever reasoned if there is a way to have a healthy relationship with a narcissist and not become one who gets frustrated? It might seem lofty and impossible to be reached. But could that be true? I will leave you to find out as you read on! And to conclude this part, will get to elaborate on how to avoid a narcissist in the most practical way. But is that all about Narcissism? Don't be too quick to say that!

Do you even know if you are a victim of the abuse? Well, there are chances that the previous chapters would have been given you hint as to what to expect; however, it is helpful to validate those feelings in this section, the fourth chapter! It begins with what your feelings might reveal what you are passing through. Next is why it can be hard to let go. You will gain deep insight into how to deal with what you have passed through. And finally, how to trust yourself again.

To wind-up, no doubt, what you would have read from the first section to the fourth chapter would have illuminated your understanding about Narcissism, but can you help yourself or anyone with the situation? Absolutely yes! The final episode will elucidate on the signs to watch to be sure you can help your partner. Additionally, you will find out a reliable treatment for anyone with a narcissistic personality disorder. And yes, you can do your best to help someone you know who is a narcissist to get over these negative traits.

I know you have a burning desire to read all. But will it not be helpful to start by explaining who a narcissist is? Keep reading to find out!

CHAPTER ONE

INTRODUCTION TO NARCISSISM

Who is a Narcissist?

Narcissist personality disorder includes a misleading self-image. In this type of trait, a person may have imbalance emotions that are so grave. Also, this trait can lead one to think or ponder excessively on positions, personal sufficiency, and prominence. Further, it has been verified that Narcissism has embedded in it the absence of fellow feeling, and an immense sense of superiority over some others.

Furthermore, a Narcissist has a high level of egocentrism. A situation where a person feels that their personal opinion, feelings, and emotions are what matters, and they will readily dismiss or discard other people's interests and ideas. People with this type of trait will have very little concern for the feelings of others. They are void of empathetic feelings. More to it is that they are always not appreciating the beliefs of others within their surroundings. No wonder researchers have validated that a Narcissist, would have an odd feeling of self-worth, and excessive preoccupation with oneself and zero lack of empathy.

With these definitions, we can dig deeper into this concept and understand some basic facts. The term Narcissist springs up from one famous character in the Greek Mythology that is named Narcissus. What happened was that he found his reflection inside a pond, and then the obsession begins. And that was when he started to fall in love with himself.

Among the list of conditions that are listed and identified as a dramatic personality disorder, a narcissist personality disorder is rated to be among one. This trait is identified with an excessive sense of self-worth.   At this point, the individual begins to feel more important; he's more focused on amassing power and attaining a high peak of success. And yet these cravings can reveal that the person has a high level of lack of self-confidence. And in fact, it can show that a person has an issue with insecurity, and low self-esteem or lack of it.

There are other several components of this behavior like excessive anger and being easily irritated. Although it has been agreed upon that for a diagnosis to be made in a person, the signs and symptoms must have to be severe and must have frequent occurrence.

As at today, statistics by the National Institute on Alcohol Abuse and Alcoholism has revealed that 7.7% of men during their lifetime would exhibit Narcissist personality disorder while 4.8% of women in today's world do the same.

However, there are varying degrees of level of Narcissist according to regions, age, marital status. For instance, it has been surveyed that folks, both men and women who are of black origin will have a higher rate of Narcissist behavior. Women who hail from the Hispanic region also have a higher rate of Narcissism. Regarding age, young adults have more chances of developing narcissist behavior than older adults. Additionally, those who are divorced or have separated from their husband or wife have a high tendency of being a Narcissist. That is not all, widows, and those who have not even gotten married will have a high rate of being a Narcissist.

Some Common Traits That Have Been Identified in Narcissist Individuals

In some individual, they have an imbalance desire or longing for the attention of others -either around them or far away from them. For some, they exhibit strong feelings of jealousy, another exhibit extreme coloring of achievements, value, and their unique talents.

In addition, some with these traits have extreme sensitivity and a high ability to be quickly hurt, and just a simple act will lead them to provocation. Sadly, these individuals also have hard times retaining delightful relationships.

Moreover, people with Narcissist trait have fantasies about their desires, Intelligence, power, and natural looks. They are ready and will quickly want to take advantage of others to reach their goal with no guilt on their conscience or feeling of remorse. People with Narcissist behavior always have the passion that only a few people can understand the stuff they're made of, their specialty and uniqueness.

They still react to criticism with vexation, humiliation, and shame. They beg for positive comments and want people to elevate them. And to them, they are comfortable with feeling that whatever they nurture and crave is the very best. Furthermore, they think that no matter what they say or did, people will certainly agree with their point or opinion.

People have classified these traits in several ways. For instance, some folks believe that these traits are a self-exhibition. Other describe these traits as being self-obsessed. Some wouldn't even describe anyone with this behavior as being tough-minded rude. Many, just like as explained earlier, maintains that anyone with this trait lacks emotion. Now, what can we conclude?

One, strictly speaking, being a Narcissist isn't right. The only advantage is meant for the person exploiting others. And on their victims, it heaps on them negative feelings and leaves them feeling depressed and sad.

While there are no special tests that can be used to confirm these traits, medical practitioners have agreed that blood tests and X-rays can shed light on ruling out the fact that other conditions can be responsible for the signs and symptoms.

In diagnosing, it must be validated that the person manipulated and took advantage of others, they always want to be admired, they have envy towards others, they think they are unique than others, others perceive their attitude as being arrogant and haughty, they fantasize about their beauty, they have the feeling that they are entitled to nearly all things.

These traits are recognized and approved by the American Psychiatric Association. Therefore, there is no question as to whether they are real or not. If any of these traits exist in you, there is no hiding; you have a Narcissist behavior. Would you agree that this is explicit enough?

So, all these are traits exhibited by Narcissist. Therefore, if you suspect that a person is a Narcissist, these will help you validate those feelings they are undergoing. How do some people get to become a Narcissist? To put it clearly, how does their background look like? Well, let's move on to the next subheading and find satisfying answers to these questions since finding a solution to narcissism demands that you understand deeply what Narcissism is all about.

Narcissism Background

Globally, Narcissistic personality disorder is now recognized as a condition that can cause extreme side effects on those they use it on. As shown from the previous subheading, you've seen that it can be identified by several symptoms like a lifestyle void of empathy, a high sense of self-worth and grandiosity.

In similarity to other types of disorder, narcissistic personality disorder includes a long-term behavioral pattern and actions that lead to multiple problems in several facets of life. These include friendship, relationship, work, and most times, family. In the U.S., for example, it has been estimated that 1% percent of adults have the traits of Narcissism, and this different disorder directly impacts them. Even though these traits aren't innate but rather it is developed over time, there is a need for us to understand the background, the origin to enhance our understanding better.

There is no doubt that Narcissism as a trait or personality has been on for many centuries; however, barely five decades ago was it believed to be an illness. Quite surprising, huh? Definitely! But we have more to learn here. To better gain further insight into this personality, knowing the origin is vital.

Did you remember where I earlier told you that Narcissist behavior springs up from? Yes, in ancient Greek Mythology. According to the myth, though, Narcissus was believed to be a proud and good-looking man. When he saw his reflection in the pool- for the first time in his life, he became drawn to himself that he couldn't even stop gazing at his beauty. And as if that was enough, he stayed staring until he passed away.

However, that isn't the only concept existing. The idea of self-admiration has long been a subject concern to several philosophers and great thinkers for quite a long time. In the time past, the idea was identified as being hubris, which is a state of extreme arrogance and pride, which eludes being far off touch of reality. But recently, it became a subject of scientific interest in the study of psychology.

Also, at the start of the 1900s, the subject of Narcissism began to invite and attracts many in psychoanalysis - a school identified for growing thought. Moreover, Austrian psychoanalyst Otto Rank reveals to the public the earliest description of Narcissism in the year 1911; the report shows that there is a connection between self-worth and vanity. Moreover, in the year 1914, the favorite Freud published a book on Narcissism. Let's get a closer look at that. Freud came up with what can even be identified as a complicated set of opinions. For the sake of knowledge, I'll share it.

He said Narcissism is linked with the inward or outward direction of one's libido (the energy that lies behind a person's instinct for survival). In his idea, he believed that infant primarily, directs their desire inward, and at that stage, he called it primary Narcissism.

Proving further, Freud claims that people experience a reduction in his so-called primary Narcissism. Also, he believed that to reduce and limit the capacity of doing it and getting back affection and love in the world would measure up to retaining a sense of satisfaction.

Moreover, Freud adds to it that a person's sense of awareness starts to develop as a child relates with the outside world and starts to learn some social norms and cultural expectations which will then lead the person to what he called ideal ego and perfect image of oneself that the pride desires to accomplish.

Also, Freud's theory suggests that the idea of loving oneself can be transferred from one person to another person. He said, when love is giving to someone, it thus affects how people experience diminished primary-Narcissism, where they are unable to develop, protect, or defend themselves. And to add more to the capacity, he suggested that receiving love and affection in return is highly vital.

But how was it recognized as a disorder? Between the year 1950s and 1960s, psychoanalysts Otto Kernberg and Heinz Kohut developed a wild interest in Narcissism. In the year 1967 specifically, Kermberg explains Narcissist personality structure. He came up with a theory that suggests the three major types: the typical adult, normal infantile, and Pathological Narcissism, which can emerge in different forms.

Additionally, in the year 1968, Kohut arrived a different understanding of Narcissistic personality disorder and moved ahead to take some of Freud's ideas. But this time, he expanded on them. In Kohut's theory, he suggested that Narcissism is a healthy and vital aspect of development, and the difficulties with self might have an influence on one's self-worth.

And in 1980, Narcissist personality disorder was finally recognized. These backgrounds of study of Narcissism has given a thorough check on how it can be understood and has helped people understand what Narcissism is down to our days. It should be noted that neither of the origins believed that Narcissism could be inherited, and that makes the point more clearly. Also, the point has given us a lead to how we can solve the problem of Narcissism. And to get to launch that we have to know how it can be developed.

Even though till today, the real causes of Narcissist personality disorder aren't known, yet some agree that parenting style has a lot to do with the impact on the child, whether the child will grow up to be Narcissist in nature or not. However, some even believe that genetics may play a role, but it has never been substantiated. It is thought that Narcissism is designed into a person's life, not before birth, but after birth. It is so severe that it can shape one's lifestyle throughout his life. But how will or do a change develop this trait? It's simple; the following points will lead the way in showing how this is established; at least four distinct points will be revealed.

How Are They Made?

Have you ever wondered? How exactly is a Narcissist personality developed? Is it an inherited trait, or it's just something that can be designed? Well, if you are keen to know, it might amaze you that researchers too have studied that and they've revealed the reasonable measure of light. It has been identified that instead of being born, Narcissist behavior is created and there are no proofs that there are Narcissist genes that can be transferred from parent to child.

Several factors can make a person develop this negative thinking and in turn, will grow and come to stay in a person's personality. To make you grasp this point better, I'll reveal the recent study that is a factor that can help one have the clear understanding to show that a Narcissist behavior isn't born instead it is being developed over time. This list will give a good clue to the development of Narcissist behavior. To attain that, I will be discussing four factors that can make a child grow up to have a Narcissist personality.

1. **When a Child is Being Overvalued.** The fact though, everyone has to be valued. If one wants to raise a child that will have a reasonable measure of self-confidence and attain an appropriate standard of self-esteem in the future, such individual needs to be valued. However, results from one study have shown that parents who excessively value their children will end up making their children rank higher in developing a Narcissist behavior as they keep growing.

If you are a parent, do you tell your kids that they are better than others, or do you often tell them that they deserve more extra features in life? If you do, in your best interest, it's better you halt that, cause if care isn't taken, you might just be training your children to use this personality on you later in the future. Instead of showering your kids with excessive praise and value, be minimal. Let young ones know that others are superior to them, and hard work is sufficient to help them get what they want.

It is noteworthy that children whose self-esteem has been reasonably built over a long period will be excited about the type of person they are, but in sharp contrast, raised self-esteem in people will make them feel like they are better off others. So, over-evaluation will undeniably lead to Narcissism.

2. **When Children Aren't Praised For Ability But Are Praised For Intelligence.** Several studies have revealed that overwhelming praise for a child's Intelligence and several innate traits will raise their level of Narcissism. So, when a child didn't work hard at getting something, and the parent showered excessive praise, they tend to develop Narcissism. Additionally, it also affects their level of contentment and drives for attending to work. So, if a parent praises a child for no actual reason, the chances there are that the child will achieve less.

On the other hand, when a parent praises a child only for hard work, and he commends only for breaking through a challenge, the child has more drive and feels a sense of achievements. Children that are told to be smart without acting will be scared of failure and wouldn't want to take the risk, thus in themselves, they develop self-defeating traits. With that, parents who want to guide the horrific attitude of Narcissism again should only teach their children the benefits and rewards that come from fighting to accomplish a task. Therefore, often praise for Intelligence instead of ability so you won't instill Narcissist traits in your child.

3. **Conditional Love**. Showing love to a kid at all time - during ups and downs is excellent for a child's upbringing. However, some parents have shielded themselves from showing this type of love. Instead, they are committed to loving their kids only when they can attain success. This is not healthy. Kids who are raised under this kind of condition are made to thrive on inconsistent attention. And their sense of identity can be affected. Their peers would impact them. They will tend to think more of themselves than others in a group. They would feel that before they can achieve something, they have to pull others down.

And that's is because, if they fail, they aren't going to find it funny, they will be humiliated, dejected and probably ignored until they achieve the aim of their parents. These feelings make the child feels that at all cost, they must win at all times. So a child with this trait will never want to entertain failure - no one should, but at times instead of letting time and unexpected event plays its part, they tear others down to help them go higher and focus on being the best.

3. **Insufficient Validation From Parents.** Aside from these factors discussed above, here is one too who shapes what a child will eventually become over time in the future. This factor is recognized as deprivation and neglect. When children do not get adequate validation from their parents, they can tend to be narcissistic. They are likely to develop an untrue picture of who they are. And when they grow old, they manage and demand that people admire them, and give them attention, which was not given to them by their parents.

Now with these four traits, let me ask you, do you think that Narcissism is innate, that is born or is it developed? Certainly, the latter. So, kids who are confined within this condition can lie to benefit themselves, they can bully others, they don't admit their mistakes. Instead, they blame others and would have an over-hyped view of themselves.

One thing is evident; it can be developed from childhood and transcend to adulthood. So, most folks you see aren't born to be Narcissist in nature; they acquired it. We still need to dig a little further into the understanding Narcissism at least to know if there is a reliable cure; that's the focus of the next subheading.

Can Narcissism be Cured?

People with Narcissism need to seek appropriate care for their condition. But how easy does it always come to admit that one has this trait or personality? It is not easy. The real-life story of a young man I will call Tom shows how difficult it could be at a time to readily admit these conditions.

Andre, for a very long time, had shown his strength as a confident man. And that is commendable. People even know him to be reasonably assured of himself. But after a while, his attitude changed. He became more inflated over minor issues, he has gotten an excessive sense of his importance and has started demand for uncalled special treatment and care.

This trait undoubtedly will have a side effect. It affects both his attitude at home and work. This began to change his life in a way he had never imagined. He was bitterly angered when he wasn't considered for promotion, which led to Jim losing his job. His closest person, his girlfriend got confused and advised he seeks professional help. At this point what do you think Andre would do? Be willing to yield to his girlfriend's advice? No! He refused and admitted that nothing was wrong with him. But something happened that pushed him to take the right step.

He noticed that his relationship with his girlfriend has started to suffer serious hiccups. But this time, reluctantly, he agreed to visit a therapist. What did Andre figure out? It was there he found out that he has Narcissist personality disorder. There is no doubt, the girlfriend's intuition has come to pass, he can no longer deny this. But one questions start to puzzle in Andres' heart. What question, you might ask?

That's the same question the theme of this subheading and the final part of this section carries. Which is: Can Narcissism be cured? Well, the fundamental truth and fact are that Narcissism is treatable, but not curable. Sad huh? Not at all! Many have been able to manage their situation using several methods that they were advised to adopt by their therapist.

The basis of Narcissist personality disorder treatment is identified as psychotherapy. And this is always the mixture of group, family, and individual therapies. They are adopted and used to know the real causes of their behavior and why they believe what they believe.

It would amaze you to know that even though narcissist behavior pushes toward the inability to show empathy. Research has shown that empathy can be learned. And if one can pick up this lesson and use it judiciously, they are better equipped in overcoming some of the effects of Narcissist personality disorder.

Additionally, through therapy, a person who is wrestling Narcissist behavior can now grow to accept responsibility for their actions. Instead of dishing blame on someone else. It would even go further by helping the person with the situation learn how to develop realistic and practical goals that will not lead to futility, which might trigger the traits. They will be helped to see how they can maintain healthy personal relationships. And these are the core goal of the therapy.

Although some have reasoned if drugs could be used in treating these conditions. But experiences from several ends have shown that medications don't always prove useful in handling the situation. However, medication can indeed help to suppress or manage a condition like anxiety and depression which go hand in hand with this condition, but there is no specific drug that can be pointed out to treat Narcissist disorder.

Noteworthy again is that changes don't come speedily. In most cases, it often requires patience on the part of those who are battling with this disorder. It demands that a person undergo an essential move in personality.

And over time, it has been validated that the best place to undergo this transition process is by using a residential mental health treatment facility. In this mode, a person is placed in an environment that wouldn't distract him, where he will be kept away from stresses and give them reliable support and designed needs. Besides, at this treatment facility, the client would receive consistent treatment for any condition that comes in connection with the disorder. They may include depression and alcohol disorder. So, at treatment and recovery center, the high level of sustainability makes it so efficient for treating the disease.

Now, if you are confident that a person you know and you love has that situation, don't feel hopeless, there is a treatment that will make the individual feel better. As long as they begin their treatment plan immediately, they are going to be better. It should be noted that there are things you can do as you even learn to help them in recovering in their situation.

The ways you can help these individuals will be discussed thoroughly in this book. Also, an in-depth understanding of various treatment plans will be revealed to you as you proceed. But don't forget that there are several types of specialist that will help a Narcissist recover from his problem. They begin with diagnosing and treating Narcissist personality disorder. There are provisions for tender and effective care in a calm and comfy atmosphere. The primary aim is to ensure that clients are keener about treatment and recovery.

The noteworthy point is that the earlier treatment plans begin, the better for the person passing through this difficulty. The better they lessen the damage done to those around them, the earlier they can yield or respond to treatment. And that means as soon as the condition is identified, a treatment plan should begin immediately.

Now that you've been convinced that there are treatment plans for those suffering from narcissist disorder, understanding the various types existing is vital and essential, it gives brighter light into the condition, and you can narrow down three types that a friend, coworker or family member is suffering from. And this might as well help you to see how you can help such an individual.

Chapter Two

Types of Narcissism

Exhibitionist Narcissism

Experiences have shown that the first thing that comes to mind when most people hear the word Narcissist are the exhibitionist. These set of people always have a constant desire to be at the core of admiring attention. Also, these set of people will ever want to overshadow conversation - they often want to feel entitled and demand that they are specially treated. They also go further in displaying that they are supremely confident, they find delight, exquisite one in relating stories and giving people advice.

But as the slightest of any insecurity, they get the GOD defense. GOD defense? I am not talking about God. Instead, this is what I mean by GOD defense. G stands for Grandiose,

O stands for Omnipotent while D stands for devaluing. Now let's expand this further to broaden our understanding.

This GOD defense is a way of explaining or analyzing the defensive, and illogical accurate facade that those who are Exhibitionist try to construct to enable them to hide their self-doubt. Rather than presenting themselves as average human like everyone with flavored talents and yes, flaws. They tend to acknowledge that they are special breed, they are perfect, and whatever they think is always right.

They go further in demanding that everyone around them agree with their point of view. In their mind, they often place themselves above others, and just a few are higher than them. Because their arrogant posture is lean and its easily pierced, and it is not how they deeply feel inside, they are easily disrupted. So even when it is a minor slight, exhibitionist narcissists are hypersensitive. They are quick to get angry and will be ready, at all times to fight over things that many people might not even take note off. Additionally, they can also be ferocious and would be void of emotion or lack emotion.

Although, they might not brag about their role, their accomplishment or relate a story where they play a significant role, yet they are everywhere devaluing others who would try to disagree with their point. For example, you might see them mock others who are within their distance. You might probably hear them say: "does he even look nice in that dress" or probably, they might even say that: "that chef is stupid" These types of people are blind to others and their feelings, their attitude, and actions which are real-life actions.

Additionally, the exhibitionist narcissist is also blind to their reasoning - they don't care if it is logical or not. These set of people doesn't get bothered and feels that everyone they discuss with must agree with their point and will immediately believe that what they are saying is exciting, humorous, or sweet.

Furthermore, the exhibitionist narcissist is insensitive and always bossy. When you disagree with them, that comes to be criticism, and it is combated with devaluation. They seek and demand progressive reassurance that they are perfect, always right and unique.

Moreover, exhibitionist narcissist attitude can be likened to a child. But how? One thing that is common among children is their look-at-me attitude. You know, generally, children have the difficulty to understand their parent's problems. So, at that stage, they have zero empathy to show towards their parents.

That is precisely how exhibitionist behaves. They have zero understanding.

Today, the exhibitionist is the stereotypical idea of a narcissist. And this is agreed by many experts today. They often think themselves to be smarter than anyone else. They have more power and are firmly convinced about that. And this trait isn't just exhibited among people that are outside their close connects. They even extend it to their friends and family. So, every time spent with them, they often feel that they are unique. Also, the exhibitionist narcissist does not have to be insecure. Carelessly, they are rude, and they will ignore or pay no attention to how their point is being welcomed. So, they practically don't see your reactions or they don't even care about it.

To better help you understand if you are having a relationship with an exhibitionist narcissist, below are the breakdown of the sections they fall into. When you spot one, you can then categorize that individual and see if you have someone who fits into that category.

1. Center of Attention.

2. Lack of Empathy

3. Expecting perfection

4. Using others

5. No apologies or responsibility

Now with these five categories, let's broaden them further.

1. **Center of attention**. They demand that the whole world revolves around them. They require care and often search for it. They expect that everyone loves and honors them. They aren't at ease in sharing spotlight with friends or other members of the family. And lastly, they are easily jealous if the attention they seek doesn't come.

2. **Lack of Empathy.** They don't understand people's feeling. They often ignore how people feel. They are capable of feeling hurt, and they don't understand and figure out when they hurt others. They only see their feelings and do not care about how others think. They are selfish. They desire that the world or those around them tend to their needs and desires. They demand everything and lack patience. And they aren't convinced that their feelings affect others.

3. **Expecting perfection.** They demand perfection from the people around them. They have an unrealistic expectation

and often have lofty standards. They believe that they are perfect, and they would not yield to correction when corrected. They push their expectations on others and decline to stay in the real world. They will move great lengths to believe that they are perfect. They will spend hours ensuring cleaning homes and buying new things. They lie to convince someone that they are perfect.

4. **Use Others**. They use family members as their props. They think people as a thing rather than considering them as people with feelings. They believe that people are easy to be changed and replaced. They can turn family members to their accessories. They push people aside to achieve their aims, and they would have difficulty sending back affection because they don't view others as equal to them.

5. **No Apologies or Responsibility**. They don't take responsibility for their actions. They fail to acknowledge that they are wrong and needed correction. They will never say they are sorry. Saying sorry is a blow to their ego, and they pretend that nothing is wrong and all is fine. They can let others suffer forever because they don't care.

With these signs, I am convinced that you shouldn't have a problem identifying an exhibitionist narcissist is. This is a guide for you. Now let's move to the second category of narcissism - closet Narcissists.

Closet Narcissist

In sharp contrast to what an exhibitionist narcissism will think, closet narcissists will be unpleasant with the fact that their positive traits are spelled out! They demand to be unique, yet they are conflicted. Right from their childhood, they have been trained that any attempt to publicly display themselves for admiration, they are going to be attacked.

This category of narcissism most times have exhibitionist father or mother who devalues them because the parent discovered that they are competition to them. You will remember that the core trait of an exhibitionist is being bossy and placing themselves over others. So, when these ones train a child, they tend to suppress them, they don't end up competing with them. They only get a reward for praising their exhibitionist narcissistic parent. So, they don't come out in public and vent their power, because those narcissistic personalities have been buried in them while growing up.

So, closet narcissists often feel insecure than Exhibitionist Narcissists. Closet Narcissists are vulnerable to enjoying the center of admiring attention. They are scared that people will see their flaws, launch an attack, and devalue them the way their parents did. Rather than showing themselves that they are unique, they instead attach themselves to people, religion, and aspects of life that they admire so much. So only by association can they feel special. Therefore, instead of telling people that they are unique and should be admired, they tend to admire others.

Closet narcissist is not openly demanding; they try to manipulate situations, so they pave the way for themselves indirectly. They are often fond of playing the victim, and they persuade people to do what they desire. In their lifestyle, they may pretend to be much more helpful than they feel deep inside. Most times, they may allow themselves to be used by others. Especially friends of theirs that are more confident than them. They live for the praise and exultation of others. And one way they get this is by working harder for them- those they admire.

So they choose someone they pick as being unique and perfect. In this person's glory, they enjoy, dine, and wine. They often imagine that some of this specialty they have or portray will be rubbed on them. From whoever they idealize, any small bit of approval and admiration is well cherished and loved. They are often linked with exhibitionist since they thought they have self-confidence which in the real sense is just defensive grandiosity.

The closest Narcissist has problem with self-doubts. If they wear a designer and people admire that on them, and it is exclusive on them, instead of admitting that, they point out to someone else. So often time they are always in search for that individual they can idealize.

Additionally, closet narcissists often behave in a more passive-aggressive way. For example, they are more likely to make their partner get frustrated at all time. They will likely say that they will do something but wouldn't do it eventually. They are doing that to avoid being kicked out of other people's reactions.

So they do what they want to do when they want to do it. And often time, they make themselves look or appear like a victim. Regularly saying one thing and then doing another will make people close to them get often infuriated. Therefore, they begin to question reality and feel deep inside them they are going nut. Closet Narcissist also can start the blame game. Where they will blame their partner for the things they didn't do, and the partner would grab and believe this because the sense of the world has become so captured. Frankly, the closet exhibition has different personas. They are bend on acting differently in specific ways. You can see them to be charismatic in public and yet with their partner, they will show cruelty and might feel even more distorted and confused.

Therefore, to narrow down their symptoms. These eight signs capture their traits and give you more critical points.

1. **Feeling Emptiness.** To cover feelings of inadequacy, those who are closet narcissist feel flawed, empty, or incapacitated when exposed to reality.

2. **Cover Up Excelling Traits**. They don't want to expose themselves to guide against the feeling of not being perfect.

3. **Failure to Express Thoughts.** Closest Narcissist who has opinions, wouldn't speak out; they prefer to meet others' expectation rather than speaking out. They tell people what they want to hear rather than what they actually mean or think.

But when angered, they can speak the truth. It often happens when at Stonewall.

4. **Impressing Others.** Rather than standing for themselves, they get to work with another person to get the person's approval so they can agree that they are perfect.

5. **They Don't Liste**n. Rather than listen to what others have to say about their character and action, probably a constructive criticism, they would yield to proving themselves or persuade others so they can see how perfect they are.

6. **The relationship is Often Void of Connection.** They are unable to retain the intimate relationship they have. They often have a problem creating a deep connection in their relationship rather than listen to their partners. As a result of that, they feel empty and wouldn't be able to develop an attachment.

7. **They Pressure Partner**. Anyone in a relationship with a covert (closet) Narcissist will undoubtedly suffer because they demand sex to make them feel special or intimate. When they don't get the privacy they crave for they feel empty and then they keep demanding for more. If they aren't emotionally fed. They pressure and seek that their needs have to be met

because they've put a lot of efforts in the relationship and they should get that in appreciation for what is being achieved.

8 Closet Narcissism Holds On. They continuously put with this to pretend that all is fine. And that everything is perfect and that can make them remain fused with their partner

Toxic Narcissist

When you need to know the most horror of the narcissistic group, then dial on toxic Narcissists. Those with the traits aren't comfortable with being the center of attraction. Instead, they want complete dominance; they desire that others tend and submit to them. In most cases, from experiences, they usually have a sadistic streak and enjoy hurting other people. What they demand from people isn't much -just obey.

We can call these set of people failed exhibitionist. And this is because they are angry that they've not been able to live up to their uncertain fantasies of limitless achievement. They go on with envying others just because they achieve what they've not made. They've stopped given up on working harder constructively and are now majorly stepping on other people's happiness and joy.

It is always not difficult to spot. Especially when they present themselves in an overt form, these include a student who finds it a delight to bully other kids who are weak and the boss in an office who desires to angrily devalue a person daily in the presence of others - in the whole office. They might call the fellow an idiot. Or say the fellow is preparing for unemployment because they are too lazy to work.

It is often easy for a toxic narcissist to reveal themselves as more covertly, and they include those who often ask difficult questions that might make a person squirm right in the presence of the whole family. They could come like why you are so thin? None of your parents were this thin while growing up as a kid. Or perhaps they could say: it's a shame that you lost your job! Can you recount the number of times you've lost your job? All these questions are to serve as an embarrassment and to weaken your self-esteem.

Their fundamental goal is to develop and place themselves as being better than other people and make those around them feel inferior and inadequate. Therefore, being with this set of people will always make you inferior and worthless. There is no way you can satisfy them; they don't praise. If you have a relationship with this person, if you get into the relationship with a moderate level of self-confidence in the relationship, after a while, your self-esteem will suffer significant damage to the extent that it will turn to self-doubt. As usual, to narrow down the signs and symptoms of a toxic Narcissist, these are what you should know.

1. **They Give Unwarranted Advice**. They do this, especially in situations where it is inappropriate. It could be about a point you've made clarifications on or on what's none of their business. When toxic Narcissists give unsolicited advice, they raise themselves above and make it feel like they are in control, and as a result, they smug. Numerous information from this fellow isn't always useful or helpful, and mostly it is being given so you can be distracted from your progressive move.

2. **They Imitate Everything About You.** If they sense that you have a trait that makes you likable and attractive, they then go ahead to mimic those traits, they want to steal your identity. In them, there exist no core sense of self. As a result of that, they prefer to mimic the qualities if yours. Your work styles, your mannerisms, and behaviors. They covet anything they can.

3. **Making You Feel Sorry For Them**. After treating you unjustly or mistreating you, they are making you say sorry. They make you want to want to tell them sorry. And even when it is evident that you aren't wrong. That way you can work harder to please them the more.

4. **They Don't Take Responsibility For Their Actions.** Only in rare cases will they take responsibility for the wrong they've done. When they apologize, it makes them feel that they are sharing in the consequences for their behavior or taking part in evolving right from it. And that's the trait of toxic people.

5. **They Verbally Abuse.** It is common for a toxic Narcissist to traumatize their partner to use that as a way to control their behavior. Toxic people believe that if they keep repeating a point consistently, you will begin to internalize it. Thereby they would be using verbal abuse to dwell as a portal to enable them to erode your identity.

6. **They are Competitive Rather Than Celebrants.** At first glance, it might be that they are going to celebrate your achievements and celebrations, but deep inside, and as time passes by, the accomplishments you reach will come under

severe scrutiny. They start to diminish those achievements as a way to feel superior.

7. **They Engage in Pathological Lying And Infidelity**. Lying comes quickly to them, and then they see nothing wrong about being a betrayal. They engage in a quite number of several affairs, and thus they can lead a double life. They have a lifestyle behind a closed door that doesn't match the life they live publicly. Thereby they engage in lying to cover up their real character.

8. **They Have Both Hot And Cold Behavior**. It could be that one minute, they are super cool, and your relationship will be on top of the roof, another minute; they are detaching themselves away from you. So, they have an alternate exchange of kindness and cruelty. One time they are cruel, the other time they are kind.

9. **They Are Judgmental.** Toxic Narcissist will often judge your life decisions. The judgment could come like a vicious attack and excessive. They step inside your life and vent their power on you.

10. **They Spread False Information About You**. Smearing lies about you becomes a thing of love. They shatter

your credibility. So even if you speak about their behavior, you'd not gain attention, because he has won you over.

What's Common Among All Forms Of Narcissism.

All these three types of narcissism discussed will always devalue other people to support their self-esteem. So they will say things to instill feelings of worthlessness into others. However, where the differences come in is who they devalue, the occurrence and the time which they devalue. Let's get more clarifications on this.

Exhibitionist Narcissists. Any exhibitionist Narcissist will always devalue other people openly, especially when they discover that they won't get the admiration they crave for. But for people they consider to be above them, they won't devalue them. They only devalue those they are competing with and those that are below their class.

Covert or Closet Narcissists. Closet Narcissists are often likely to devalue themselves rather than devaluing others. Frequently, they will apologize, and if they are devaluing other people, it will undoubtedly be behind closed doors. They might publicly express envy but will never insult or demean others publicly.

Toxic Narcissist. For this category of people, they are often delighted in seeing that others are squirming in embarrassment. Starting an interaction by putting them down is their goal. It might be mildly, openly, or bluntly. Toxic Narcissist often leads to devaluation.

Conclusion on The Three Forms of Narcissism.

From this in-depth understanding, have you come to see that all forms of Narcissism are not all similar? Some could be toxic; for others, they can be covert while some could still be exhibitionist.

So, Narcissists use others to heighten their self-esteem. But now if you are sure from this highlighted point that you are in a relationship with a Narcissist, how can you avoid them or deal with them? The next section is designed to help you see what you can do to halt the impact a Narcissist can have on you.

CHAPTER THREE

AVOIDING AND DEALING WITH A NARCISSIST

Narcissists Techniques And How Narcissist Manipulate

Form the previous knowledge; you aren't a newbie to the traits and characteristics of a Narcissist. The Narcissist is known for being a manipulator. They have different techniques that they employ alongside their habit to make their wish come to reality. This section will discuss how you can avoid a Narcissist.

However, it is good to begin with the techniques and how they use them on their bait. Being exposed to their techniques will bring profound understanding into getting the message on how they can be avoided.

To have a broader knowledge. I'll discuss 15 unique techniques that are being used by Narcissist individual.

1. **Gaslighting**. This is one of the conventional techniques adopted by a Narcissistic individual. This technique can be described in several ways. I will use three sentences in describing this. These are: That didn't happen. It's your imagination, and are you crazy?

Further explanation is identified by most scholars today to be the most insidious manipulative techniques that exist in the realm of narcissism. The function it serves is to work out distorting people's view and their sense of reality. It takes away one's ability to trust his or her instinct and come to a reasonable conclusion. Also, when you have the feeling of not being justified, even when being maltreated or abuse, you don't often know how to loosen yourself and how to reject the idea thrown at you.

For instance, when a Narcissist says its only your imagination. They are making you feel like the reality eludes you and you have a distorted view of the fact that exists in the realm of any individual. Or when they say you are crazy. They heap on you the feeling that you have either mental disability, nor you lack a sense of right and wrong.

2. **Projection.** You have seen that a toxic Narcissist will never admit that the madness that is happening around him is all his fault. Instead, they push the blame on you, sometimes out rightly. That technique is what is identified as a projection. Although you might have even done that sometimes ago, and I can attest to the fact that I have done it before - we are all guilty.

But where it becomes a habit is when one makes it a pattern. And that is the Narcissist techniques. And it even goes deeper than that.

By projection, the person is displacing responsibility of one's negative behavior and traits and thus attribute it to another person who is closer to them. They could even assign it to someone else. Take, for example, if they got to a meeting late, they might claim that the timing is terrible, it should be adjusted. Instead of blaming their inability to meet up with the time they turn the table. This technique can make people around these individuals feel an imbalance, unstable, and have the feeling of not doing things right at all time, which in reality might not be accurate.

3. **Generalization**. This is another technique that is being employed by anyone who is a Narcissist. Let's take this example for closer understanding. Let's assume that at your workplace, you told a coworker that he sometimes fails to take into consideration the long-term ramifications of individual decisions. But that office Narcissist claims that you have dubbed him a loose cannon. You speak further and tell him that if this situation keeps on like this, it might lead to a disaster. But your Narcissistic colleague flared up and said you called him a disaster.

Do we say he doesn't understand where you are aiming at? No, he does, but he's just too lazy intellectually. Instead of taking time to analyze the situation and look at it at every perspective, he generalizes issues - whatever you say, and don't recognize the senses in your logical reasoning. Neither will he take into account different perspective. Even if you are thinking intellectually and ensure that he puts his intellect into work, he fails and wouldn't mind being an intellectual mastermind. And if one isn't careful, you might be pushed to shift the truth in fear and also admit the generalization.

4. **Moving The Goal Posts.** This is a logical fallacy, and using it is typical of Narcissists. They do this to make sure that they own all the reasons in this world to be perpetually dissatisfied with you. And this happens even when you've presented all the logical evident backing a specific claim. Or they take an action that will meet up with their request. They continually set up questions for you. In fact, in another way, they might even request for more proofs from you, and by proofing further, they are getting the liberty to shift blame.

Take, for example; when you decide to act in line with the company's policy and you've done your best to meet up with the standard, they might come to fault your attitude and show that you've accomplished nothing noteworthy by the firm, or you have to validate the claim further using more proofs to do that. The more you try to prove yourself, you end up feeling a sense of unworthiness, and each time you think, whatever you think is not right to them. Thus, he will achieve his aim, which is to lower self-esteem and for you to fear them when attending to your duties.

5. **Switching Subject.** This technique used by Narcissist has been useful for quite a long time. It hasn't stopped and it still been used today. Although, you might think that what's

the harm in switching conversational topics, but in the hands of a manipulator, they do that to help them avoid accountability or do away with taking responsibility for their actions. They wouldn't want people to hold on to a topic that will make them accountable for anything. To achieve that, they will reroute the subject to fulfill their benefit.

Unfortunately, this can go on for a very long time even forever if you are not conscious, and it will silence the discussion of issues that matter. And do not forget that the more you allow irrelevant debate, the more you ignore the pressing one and then you can't speak on the issue that needs urgent attention. Be reminded that they are doing this at your own detriment and not precisely to your favor. The more the conversation keeps going, he digs out your flaws and makes you feel more worthless. Therefore, staying focused on the real subject is indeed the route to win the war against a Narcissist.

6. **Name - Calling**. This can seem subtle, but trust me, it is destructive. And as subtle as it is, it can quickly pierce through and make you feel worthless, and you entertain all manner of names. It can go on and on until it gets to a stage where you will not be able to tolerate it. That means you have to stop it.

They may start by calling you a name that was as a result of what you didn't do right. It gets to the world, and everyone starts to look at you in that light, what they readily think about you is the name, and not that it diminishes your ability to concentrate on your duty. Then you will be scared of what people will think and how they will feel about what you do; they are influencing how you view yourself.

Another thing that name-calling reveals about narcissism is that they have deficient in reasoning in a higher-level method. And they want to use you as their playground to be a king in their lower state. Surprisingly, it can happen anywhere. It can even happen in the official political positions too.

7. **Smear Campaigns**. Well, you've heard of smearing lies as being a trait of those who have Narcissistic behavior. But how do they use this technique on others?

First is, they try to see if they can halt the way you view yourself. But when that one can't be accomplished. What they do next is playing the martyr, and that makes them label you as a toxic person. This campaign is identified as a preemptive strike that will be used to sabotage your reputation and make sure that they slander you wherever they meet themselves.

The campaign can make many groups divides themselves, some agreed to the lies, others refute the claim. And this can even happen among Intelligent individuals. Sad yet if this gets to you, it might end up sabotaging your reputation too. And this will keep your status at great jeopardy.

They can be so crafty hat the smearing campaign will be believed at first sight. They might bring one flaw of yours and give a distorted view about you making it seems as if you've been doing that a long time. And even if you aren't refuting the claim Intelligently, they will win.

8. **Devaluation**. You aren't new to this, but one thing about devaluation is that it begins with love for you and the person who occupied the position you now hold will be wrongly reported on by the same person. They might start by commending you and feign that they see sense in what you've done in contrast to what the person that was holding the position did.

Let's pick an example. The person occupying the position you are now holding had sometimes sanctioned or sacked some employee for acting cruelty. But when something like that happens during your time, you gave a strong warning and added that it should never repeat itself. Now a Narcissist might not get to see if the cases are weightier than each other. They might start to devalue their former colleague to elevate you. But if you begin to fall for this, what they did to the former colleague will be used on you. Yes, over time you won't have to doubt this again.

9. **Aggressive Joke.** We should all have a reasonable sense of humor. And a narcissist will not revolve around this healthy sense. Instead, he would want to hide under that and launching cutting jokes that is aggressive to the person he is aiming it at.

For example, covert Narcissist would find and derive joy in making very blatant and malicious jokes at the expense of your integrity. After saying it, they might then say "it's just a joke" doing that will now make them get away with the uttering of those appalling words. And while they even do that, they might act to be calm and innocent. If you try to show that those remarks are not proper and not healthy, they will fight back by saying you lack a moderate sense of humor. Which isn't correct.

As you contemplate this, you might even be thinking if what happened was just little innocent fun. It's a blatant lie. The joke is aggressive. They are firing that so they can bruise your confidence and let you doubt your judgment. It is often common among friends and especially coworkers. They might try this on you. You have to be able to identify what bruises your self-confidence and decipher which humor is simply humor. Although in most cases, when the joke hurts you, it could be a sign.

10. **Triangulation**. This has proven to be one of the smartest tactics by Narcissist folks. They aim at distracting you from their flaws and then focus you on the probable threat of another person. And that is why it is called triangulation.

The techniques involve the love of reporting back falsehoods about what others have said about you. And yet, the person they are reporting the statement to you would have been manipulated to have arrived at this conclusion. The person is only a victim and not likely an enemy of yours.

But a Narcissist might make it seem like the person is your enemy. So paying too much attention to what "they said" might turn a "manipulated" person into an enemy. And who has succeeded in making that work? It is the manipulation by the Narcissist, using the triangulation techniques.

11. **Shaming**. One thing about life and our lifestyle is that we will never have everything. And that truth has come to be

one of the playgrounds of narcissists. They may begin with what they see that you lack. And use it to shame you. Let's take two examples.

A Narcissist might pick your lack of a degree. Even if you have a high level of exposure coupled with a wide range of experience, a Narcissist might fault your reason in a public setting where you and him stand an argument and shame you with the fact that you don't own a degree and had it been you've got a degree you would have been able to understand his line of reasoning.

Another example is your appearance. Are you a fellow that isn't really up to date will latest fashion trend yet you still dress moderately? A Narcissist might snap at and use your lack of high-class dress sense as a weakness against you.

The Narcissist is always on the road to belittle whoever comes their way as well as they see or sight anything that seems unacceptable to them to shame an individual they are using it on.

12. **Brainwashing**. This is one of the psychology techniques for manipulation, but undeniably, Narcissists are an expert in this field too. Initially, you might maintain a stand

that you aren't going to do a particular task or attend to duty, but unconsciously you find yourself doing it. You've been brainwashed.

What they use in achieving this is by plotting you to get you to obey their commands even though you don't desire to do that. For instance, they might start by explaining the financial benefits that would come if you can take up this task. Or perhaps they start to give examples of people who didn't toil with an opportunity and made big waves in the economy. And all this is to their advantage, and when you start to do, they command you and before you get to know you've become their pet that they can toss up and down as they wish.

13. **Inappropriate Behavior.** A narcissist regularly behaved more like an extroverted person. They have been reported to use more sexual languages often. As a result of that, they tend to humiliate you in public. And then you will even have to apologize to them for their behavior - inappropriate one at that.

Also, that action is pushed at you so you can help boost their ego and enhance their relevance. And when that is lashed at you, you are more likely to help them smooth things over, and they will get away with unacceptable behavior.

Inappropriate behavior in narcissism is often offensive and could be cruel to your personality. Often time they use sexual languages as a basis to start and bring your confidence down. Before you know you have been manipulated. In this case, one of the best things to do is identify where a conversation is heading to and notice the primary motive. You can by paying attention from the beginning and critically think about what is being said before you will be drawn into the conversation. You might be doing yourself good by removing yourself from that situation, so you can still maintain your confidence.

14. **Inability to Control Emotions.** When Narcissists have difficulty controlling their emotion; then it may lead to physical aggression. And in some instances, they might start by intimidating to make you feel fearful, they might go on to threaten you, and from there it might lead to using denigrating languages. These languages will be applied to you to demean you. Does it end there?

There venting of anger might lead to withholding their support. This support could be physical, financial, and emotional. They are doing this to make you feel that they are being hurt by a seemingly wrong act.

If you are in a relationship with a Narcissist, for example, if it is your husband or your wife, they might use this technique by restricting your access to friends and family. They could even be at the forefront of your behavior. And will also pressure you heavily so you can do what you didn't want to do at the initial stage. This attitude might get a person fearful, and what he could be needing at that point is how to ensure safety. And this type of attack can even lead to domestic violence - a situation that might cause trauma.

15. **Playing Victim**. This, being the last technique used by Narcissist, is worthy of mention. This technique has the attitude that will enforce you to sympathize with them so their ego can be justified.

Often time you hear them say, "I can't win with you." Deep down, they know you have a strong stance. Doing this will make them want to let you back down. That way you can let them go, have everything at their disposal.

These 15 different techniques are used employed by narcissists. They are all on a rampage today, at work, in school, family and even with friends.

But evidently, you can avoid the situation, and in fact, control some of their influence. That is, some of the impact they have on you. But how can you do this? Well, before I proceed on to that, I'd love to introduce to you how you can peer into your relationship and examine if you've been a victim of this so you'll get treatment. They are the tips that will help you validate your claim and bring things to perspective; then it will prepare you to understand what you can do to avoid them.

How A Relationship With a Narcissist Looks Like

Are you a husband, wife, or a son or daughter to someone? How would you finally conclude that you are in a relationship with a narcissist? Even though the pattern adopted in a Narcissist relationship might want to look similar to the techniques discussed above, this section focuses more on how it's been carried out in a relationship and the pattern you would be able to relate with which will clear your doubt or reinforce your conviction that your relationship isn't narcissistic in nature. Ten unique models will be discussed, and to what end? To cover it broadly.

1. **Little or No Permission to Talk About Yourself.**
For example, if you are a wife in the house, how often are you being allowed to express your views? Hardly or you can't even remember the last time it happened? Then the chances are high that you are with a Narcissist. A Narcissist talks about himself or herself more than allowing others to talk about themselves. They frown at a two-way conversation. And in this type of relationship, you struggle so that you can have your views tendered. But even if you now have the opportunity to speak up about your feelings. Guess what will happen? You might be criticized, ignored, or you are going to be corrected.

If you are a son, do you often get replies to your views like 'but,' actually and you see, there is more to it that you can see! You can always sense that he feels and acts like he knows better than you. There is no doubt that you are in that type of relationship.

2. **You Get Interruption Often Times**. Don't mistake this for the poor communication skills that some may have; they simply interrupt, and that doesn't stop them from listening to the person's view later on. But what the person you are in a relationship will do is to interrupt and take the lead in the conversation, worse yet, he will turn the attention of the

conversation to himself. And you can spot that he has no genuine interest in you, can you be wrong about this, no!

Take for instance, when was the last time you are trying to tell your spouse how you were given brilliant commendation at work, and he snatched it and started relating what he underwent at work that day and how he won people's approval. This isn't appealing. You are correct.

3. **He Breaks Rules**. Even though minute, they seem not to care. For example, does your family make rules about what should be done if anyone presses his or her phone before the end of a meal? What happens, does he or she breaks the rule and want to get away with it? Is there any rule concerning the use of a TV set in your household? How does he or she respond, favorably? Or he has never abode by it? You see, in a Narcissist relationship, they are interested in violating rules and some norms.

Another aspect of breaking rules that need to be watched in a rule breaker is stealing people's properties - particularly office supplies. They've never kept to the appointment. And how often does he break traffic laws while you were going for an event? The fact though, we feel remorse for whatever wrong we've done, and wouldn't want to get back to it, but a Narcissist knows that what he has done is wrong, he wouldn't apologize, neither will he feel remorse.

4. **Don't Maintain Boundaries.** Yes, we all have feelings, emotions. And to people in a relationship, it is highly vital that their feelings and emotions are taken into considerations, but they will not. Instead, they will overstep and use you and would not be sensitive to your tastes and concerns.

How often does your spouse break promise he made and will never leave up to his obligations? And top of it you are not accorded any form of respect, and if you complain about that, you are charged that you are to be blamed for that. Have an arrangement; what you hear is that, you are the reason why I did forget. I'd not have forgotten if you had reminded me.

5. **Image Pretense.** Ask yourself, does the way you are being treated in public have a vast difference from the way you are being treated in private. Any difference? They act like they are angles outside, and then they launch their devil mood at home. Worse yet, even if they will agree to do something with you, how does he do it? Probably he or she is doing that to tell you that they are better than you, they are telling you that they are unique than you and many more.

6. **They Feel Entitled**. How does he or she expect you to treat him? Give him preferential treatment, and you'd never get a small fragment in return. They think that the world revolves around them and that you have to think more about them than they will think about you?

7. **They Are Persuasive.** Do you only get loved when it's time for sex and when they need your favor? Then, when the phase is over, they are likely to switch back to their initial mode, and you get used eventually. In their mind, within that moment when they need you, you get their attention, the next second, you are so disgusting that you don't need to be reckoned with.

If your parent or your spouse often engage you only when they need to fulfill their desires and would demand that you give him full attention, you are definitely in a Narcissist relationship.

8. **Grandiose Personality**. Has he or she ever told you that you can't live without him or probably he feels that without him you can't survive? The spouse needs each other to complement their love, but putting up action that makes you feel like you are worthless is a blow on your confidence. If you are both working on a project, the success isn't shared. Instead, they take glory for the success of the project.

9. **Negative Emotions**. Although in a relationship, they might needlessly not spread what is wrong about you to people - they do too, just that it has a limit. But in the home, they give you tantrums if you dare go against their wish or you don't agree with their opinion. And you don't dare correct him or her; they fire back.

If your spouse regularly and quickly results in judging you and ridiculing you in public, they are indirectly making you feel inferior. They boost their fragile ego by making you feel inferior.

10. **Always At The Head Of Decision -Making.** Have you ever been allowed to make Decision even though minute? They are still at the edge of making a decision. That's not all; they also proceed to make a decision that will soothe them with no consideration for who you are and what you stand for. You must bow to their rules and regulations, and you aren't allowed to drop your view.

A relationship with a Narcissist is profoundly evil and not the best. It has the potential to gradually kill and render a person inactive over a long period. Now can you see yourself in a relationship with a Narcissist? Fine! The following points will help you know how you can avoid that situation without causing any havoc to yourself or the Narcissist!

How to Deal With A Narcissist And Avoid Their Negative Impact on You

Being in a relationship with a Narcissist isn't healthy. Even though they are complicated, sensitive, and have a very high degree of self-esteem, it doesn't mean that they can't be stopped or they cannot be won over.

Below, I've outlined not just the theoretical aspect of dealing with a Narcissist. The following points are practical suggestions that can be adopted in dealing with a Narcissistic person and placed in it, are signs that will help you when its time to move on because they can be verbally and emotionally abusive.

1. **See Them For Who They Are**. When they desire to, those who have Narcissistic behavior are perfect in turning on the charm. And unconsciously, you might find out that you are attached to their ideas and promises. And in the work settings, they might just be known as being fashionable.

However, before you are being attached or drawn into that scene, take a careful look at how they treat people when they are on the stage. If you find out that they are lying, or are disrespecting others, or they are manipulating others, don't swallow the pill that it won't get to you; it surely will!

Don't just fall for whatever they say or do; it doesn't matter to them; what counts and matter to them is how they will end up using you. So, pay no attention to what they say and do. Instead of contemplating and thinking whether they will change or thinking that it is just a coincidence, don't be fooled, believe what you see on the stage! Accepting them for who they mark the first step to dealing and avoiding them. And there is no much you can do about their attitude.

2. **Shatter The Spell And Don't Pay Attention to them**. Regardless of the attention they seek to have, negative or positive, those who have Narcissist attitude will always do all they can to ensure that they remain in the spotlight. If you aren't careful, you might be buying into their tactics. Unknowingly you will be pushing your needs apart to satisfy them.

You might have this wrong belief that you will soon break free from their attention seeking behavior and thus you can tolerate it for the first time, the fact is, that time will never come. Regardless of how much time you spend adjusting your lifestyle to suit them, it will never be enough. But what can be done?

Don't allow them to sabotage your sense of self. That is who you are and what you stand for, don't let them define your world. You did matter and then regularly tell yourself that, if you do, it reminds you that you are to be considered too regardless of what they think or do.

And you can do that by reminding yourself of your strengths, goals, and desires. So be in charge. Always tell yourself that you are also entitled to some "me time" often take care of yourself, and it is never your responsibility to fix them.

3. **Speak Up For Yourself**. Although the idea of walking away on some things and ignoring will be the best thing to do, with a Narcissist, it doesn't have to be all the time. In most cases, you will be required to speak up.

You have to consider the settings. The way you will speak up with a boss will be different from your spouse and your parent or co-worker or even your friend. So, you have to consider and put the environment into perspective.

Some individuals with Narcissist personalities appreciate using others, and if you are getting that, endeavor not to display annoyance because if you do, you will only be fueling their arrogance and pride. If the time you spend with this one isn't significant and you don't hope to have a prolonged relationship with him, you will need to keep boundaries.

But if it is a person you will like to keep within your circle, then you will need to speak up. But always do it calmly and gently. You need to show them how their words and actions impact your life. And don't beat around the bush, instead be specific and be clear about how you wish to be treated. And be ready for the fact that they might agree or not.

4. **Set Clear Boundaries**. It isn't new to you that a Narcissist person enjoys being self-absorbed. And so, like I said earlier, situations matter, but how do you initiate the boundary.

If they are trying to get into your space or your private life, they don't even see those boundaries that you set for yourself. And more importantly, you have to set boundaries.

If you have a co-worker who snoops into your chats and intrudes into a phone conversation you had with someone, you can politely tell the person you can handle it, and you don't want him or her to intrude. Don't stop there; state the consequences.

For example, you can say, when next he does it, you might snub him, and that wouldn't be fair. You'd be surprised that they won't disrespect your choice. That's the boundary. If it is your boss, limit some conversation to the office and don't go beyond. You might even tell them that you won't be comfortable speaking on that subject and don't give him a chance to speak further. Politely thank him and walk away.

5. **Be Ready For a push Back**. Do you think someone who thinks they want to bruise your ego and you end up doing that would be happy about it and wouldn't fight back? That won't happen. So be ready.

Some of the things that you should be ready for is that they might come with their demand. And they might even come back to want to make you feel guilty or make you believe that you are just unreasonable and you are controlling; don't give in, it's merely a play for sympathy. But when those periods come, be ready to maintain your decision. If you don't keep that, they won't take you seriously the next time you try that.

6. **Remember That The Fault Isn't Yours.** If a Narcissist hurts you, they won't want to take responsibility. Take, for example, if it is coming from your spouse, he or she might want to push the blame on you and switch responsibility.

You might be pushed to keep the peace and then take the blame. But you don't have to lower yourself nor judge yourself. Instead, stand on the truth that you know and don't switch off from the fact. Don't just let anyone take the truth away from you.

If he's late for an event and he pushes the blame on you, tell him that's not true and try to bring our where his fault lies. Don't be scared, speak up. When you are fully convinced of the truth, don't hide it. Speak out and be observant to take note of every situation so you can understand where the wrongs are coming, and the faults are gathering up.

7. **Get a Support System**. Most times, how we avoid a Narcissist might differ from one situation to another. Reducing your closeness with a workmate will differ from your spouse or the relationship between a parent to their children. But what can help if you're dealing with a Narcissist that is your spouse?

Build up your healthy relationships and firmly support network of kind and humble people. If you don't, it might drain you drastically. So, is there is an old friend that cherishes you so much, can you try and call this one and rekindle of your relationship?

Also, raise new ones that don't have the threat of leading to a Narcissist relationship. Get together with family more regularly. And if you want to expand your circle more, you can pick up classes. If there is any charity work that can be done in your community, don't hesitate to join in. Engage in what will make you meet new people and feel comfortable. This helps you relieve emotions, boosts your self-confidence, and increase your joy.

Remember that a healthy relationship involves listening to each other and effort to understand each other, both individual agree to their faults and take responsibility for them, and they both feel that they can enjoy themselves in the front of others.

8. **Don't Dwell On Promises, Prioritize on Immediate Action.** You already know that those who are Narcissist make promises and would always fail. They wouldn't tell you they will do those things you hate but will promise to do those ones you want. And generally, they promise to do better.

It might even come with sincerity, but the truth is that the promise is a means to an end. As soon as they get what they want, then the motivation is gone, and you won't be able to match their actions with their words.

In that case, the best thing to do to get out of that feeling is that you stand on your ground, demand for what you need and stand on it. Maintain the stand that you will only fulfill their wish only when they attend to yours. Be consistent, because that is what will help you to stand on your point and not give in to their tactics. And before you know it, you have arrived at your need.

9. **Believe That He May Need Help Professionally**. People having a Narcissist problem might not be willing to seek professional help because they don't see themselves having a problem.

It has also been experimented that those who are narcissist might also have an additional disorder. This may include mental health or personality disorder. And this might be a reason to seek help.

Therefore, you might be kind enough to tell them to seek professional help. But don't forget that you can't force them to do it. Instead, it is their responsibility, and you have to admit that. Even though the Narcissist trait is a mental condition, that isn't an excuse for bad behavior.

10. **Identify Your Need For Help Too.** You can affect your own mental and physical health if you regularly deal with a Narcissist. Thereby you might need help if you sense that you are living with a Narcissist. But how would you know that you need help?

If you have symptoms of depression, anxiety, and you can't explain a particular physical ailment. Head on to see a doctor. As soon as you are being checked, there might be a referral to other services like a therapist and support. Call in family and close friends to be part of your support system. You don't have to deal with it alone.

But what should you do if a Narcissist is becoming verbally or emotionally abusive? Below are signs that you can watch out for in an abusive relationship.

- If they start to call you to make and rain insults on you.

- If they begin to yell on you and threaten to beat you

- If they accuse you or are overly jealous

- Blaming you for everything that goes wrong

- Monitoring your movements

- Denying things that are obvious to you.

- It is best to walk away from the relationship if:

- You are verbally or emotionally abused.

- You feel controlled and manipulated

- You are being abused physically

- He or she shows signs of mental illness

- Your mental health has been affected

If you conclude leaving the relationship, don't delay seeking professional help. But how does the healing process of a Narcissist look like? Why might it be hard for you to leave the relationship, what might your feeling show? If you are a victim, can you get back on track and still trust a future relationship? **Moving to the next section, you will come to** find answers to those questions.

CHAPTER FOUR

HEALING PROCESS

What You Will Go Through

If you have confirmed that you have been a victim of a narcissist, and you want to break free, you will need to understand what you will go through during the healing process. There is no doubt that you will undergo series of emotional trauma, and these traumas are what I want to discuss so that as you heal on, you wouldn't think it is a lost cause to embark on this stage.

These experiences are normal feelings, and they are signs that show that things are getting better and will eventually get better. However, do note that you may not experience them in order of arrangement, yet you can't do without undergoing any of the emotions that will fall in this category that will be mentioned.

1. **Anxiety**. A narcissist naturally wants to be the one to discard, he wants to be the one that will reject you, or he will continually beg that you shouldn't let go because a narcissist hates to hear "no." However, irrespective of how it happened, ending it will undoubtedly be hurting and painful. And where the anxiety falls in is when you don't know whether he will still find his way back and want to get you on in the relationship. Over time, he has been seen as a big part of your life, and that end that seems sudden may overwhelm you. But don't feed on that. Just believe in yourself that it is over, and it is over. Be ready to speak up if he or she ever contacts you. Don't forget; you have to be decisive and maintain your boundary, that way you can keep your anxiety at bay.

2. **Obsession**. It will be possible that as you back out of that relationship, you will begin to get a hard time concentrating. In your head, you have in their plenty of questions that you don't even have answers to. You might ask a question like did he really love you? Was he even aware that he hurts me, could it be that he was doing it out of love? Am I not even wrong? Is there a way I would have helped the

relationship from falling apart? Which parts of the relationship prove to be real? How could he have moved on so quickly? And so many questions!

There is the tendency that you will want to go over everything that happened again; you will even want to reroute and see what you would have done to let the relationship works. So you will begin to formulate plans in your head thinking if you had done that it would have been better. These are simply obsession; they don't identify the real picture. It is a stage, and you will overcome it, give it time, and there you go!

3. **Grief**. This is even worse than an obsession. Because you are likely to feel despair and this will continually overwhelm you each time you try to think about the close-knitted bond you had with such individual - your ex or a close friend. And you can't help but miss him. You will also have to think that the relationship you had with him was one of the most genuinely romantic relationships you could ever think of, which has never happened to either you or your family relatives. Yes, it might even happen that you will think that you can never have such again.

It might even go intense that you will start to think that you never thought well and your instincts weren't right. So, in most cases, your grieving comes in two folds. First, you will have to grief about your ex leaving you and the loss of the relationship, the second type of grief is the one you will always remind yourself that you will have done things better which in another way round translates that you do not have a real understanding of what happened in your relationship. It is safe to say that at that stage, you are clouded and are far from reality.

4. **Loneliness**. I'm pretty sure you'd have envisaged this even before calling it quit. The pattern that the abuse takes is to let you find it had to describe, and you will have a hard time understanding what happened. Even if you have to seek advice, it seems as if they don't understand your feelings and your thinking. Also, if someone moves to you and tries to know what you are passing through, there are high chances they won't understand.

This inability to understand you isolate yourself and feel like you need to be alone a particular time. Thinking that you are left alone with your experience and there is no one to talk to, in fact, you might feel like withdrawing from several social activities that would have helped in boosting you properly or assisting you in getting over. Your clouded judgment at this point will not let that happen, and instead of that, you will keep focusing on yourself, the relationship, and your ex. Doing this will even make you grief the more and increase your bitter feelings, and that will do you more harm than good.

5. **Doubt**. Everyone who is undergoing a stage of recovering from the hand of a narcissist will feel a high level of uncertainty. Take, for instance, has there ever been a time when he admitted the wrong he did, and he readjusted his attitude. How often? Maybe you can think of one or two occasions. How about other periods? Sadly, your brain wouldn't think of those periods; instead, your mind will think about the coincidental acts of kindness. You will never think of those times the blames dashed on you even when it is evident that it is never your fault. Those times too, your angry reactions and outburst of anger were dubbed by him as the root cause of the problem.

You won't remember being name called, being attacked to be jealous. Instead, you will start throwing guesses. Like you are making a mountain out of a minute issue, as if all was your fault, worst of it all, you doubt if your ex is a narcissist. Many had undergone this period later confess to the fact that after the period passes away, they were able to put the matter in perspectives.

6. **Shame**. At the tail end, when you are trying to attain final recovery, you might begin to think that why would you have allowed someone to take advantage of you that long. He hurts you on several occasions; you were being manipulated and controlled. You passed through a series of insecurities, you were embarrassed in public, yet you kept your cool, and you were together until you got exposed to the understanding of what being a narcissist is all about. To have the shame even the more, you wondered that he might be right. Maybe all he said was right that you are genuinely worthless. All these thoughts make you feel ashamed of yourself. You begin to think that you are the owner of those attributes and you start to criticize yourself even for what you couldn't get control over. Speaking in public becomes a thing of fear because you don't know if all he said about being outspoken is true. Even though you might not be right at all times in the relationship, you are not to be blamed about the misfortune that happened.

7. **Anger**. The combination of shame, doubt, and anxiety, and even sadness will start to dwindle; then you begin to acknowledge that you have been used and manipulated. Then what happens next? Anger! You will start to let yourself feel so angry over the pains and series of suffering that you were made to pass through. Now they are getting more apparent to you,

it's not an illusion again and rather than feeling like retracing your steps back and make things work, you feel like getting back and deal with the Narcissist.

It gets so severe that you start to think that the relationship even suppresses some of the pains and anger you were denied when the relationship was on. It irks you. Further, you want to lay your hands on the devil called your ex but it's not within reach.

And at the stage, denial isn't something of consideration. This is real! You might start seeing the stabs, the marks of pain that were fired at you, and you weren't on the know. You will want to call on some friends to hear you out and suggest how you can pay back

8. **Relief.** Yes, that time will come. After all, as you move farther off the Narcissist, the toxic feelings install in you begin to fade. You no longer blame yourself, but you blame the Narcissist. Then gradually, the heaviness in your heart starts to melt. You no longer feel that if you aren't with him, you can't enjoy life. As a result, your heart begins to clear off. Then the world starts to make more sense to you once again. You feel that the thought of going back to him is evil and unwarranted.

Then the process begins thoroughly; you convince yourself that you have a long way to go, but something unusual occurs, you say to yourself that you will go over this, and you surely will work towards that. Well, as you heal on, you might come to realize that there is no way you'd have to erase the story like it never happened, but you will have the conviction that you will get better and now allow the relationship to stand to be what it is now, an unfortunate one to you. This makes you feel more relieved, and you wish you knew this before now. And you quickly want to get yourself into any plan that will reveal your true self the more.

9. **Focus On Yourself**. More importantly, you begin to realize that you have to focus on yourself. You might start by trying a new hobby or visiting a gym center. At first, it may be daunting and timid to start associating with new friends because a Narcissist would have drained or sapped your energy. But realizing you are out of the situation will give you a boost. You will get more desire to reconnect with people that have sometimes made you happy and that you'd want to make them happy too.

Then you will realize how aside you were pushed and your emotional needs weren't met, and you couldn't stand the relationship that will come in that format again in your life. In trying to focus more on your life, you are not eager to jump into any form of relationship; instead, you want a healthy relationship - one that will focus on both parties and not one-sided. You are convinced that you will get that and that only patients can let you do that. You know you still need more, so you begin to search.

10. **You Will Get Someone New.** Although you will have to undergo a series of lessons (all we will be discussed later) that will help you regain and get to be who you are before you finally get back to this stage. But when you do, you will be happy you did. You will now search for the qualities that will make you get the right person, and that a healthy relationship is more about two people having the same goals and understanding each other, no name calling not emotional or physics abuse.

It is just more fun, and you would find out that it's great to recover finally. With that stage comes comfort and freedom! You can't trade it. But wait, do you even wish to know why it is hard to let a Narcissist go? You may likely have wondered. Well, many have done that too, but it seems like there is no answer, but there are answers. Those answers will shed more light on how to back out easily before things start to fade off.

Why it is Hard to Let go

Narcissists form a powerful bond with whoever is their partner. And it can be challenging to break. Experiences have shown that it takes more than 2-3 times to succeed finally. But don't worry, you don't have to do it repeatedly before you break free. Below are why it is hard, and once you understand that, you are off their chains.

1. **A Narcissist mimics You to Become Your Perfect Partner.** During the love bond phase at the start of the relationship, a Narcissist would want to learn many things about you. He starts by learning what you desired and then mirrors it back to himself. Thus, he can develop a psychological environment where you will begin to develop a deep, secure attachment. They flatter you excessively and often time reassures you that they will meet your deepest insecurities. Their primary goal is just to let you drop your guard, and then you are vulnerable to them. So, you are firmly attached to them which can't shake.

2. **They Don't See The Relationship Ending.** A Narcissist might think the relationship to be temporarily on a pause mode if they are attending to another person or they are angry. But they are never done breaking up with you. So, in their feeling, they feel that you belong to them, and you are going nowhere. And they are the one to decide when to enter and back out of the relationships. They make it a repeated attempt to ensure that you break any no-contact plan you are building.

3. **You Are Bombarded With Questions**. Indeed, there will be so many things you won't understand in the relationship. You would start asking if he truly loves you, and when trying to figure out all those questions you are still stuck on the relationship, instead of manning up and giving yourself the boost to call it quit, you will think that it will get better and that and you will get answers to all your questions, and this will delay you further, assuming that you will only be relieved when you get reply.

4. **You Develop a Chemical Bond With Him.** The bond that exists between you and the narcissist is a chemical bond. Where it revolved between kindness and wickedness. And that might make you start feeling withdrawal symptoms

and dependence that weren't your fault at first. This addiction is capable of drawing back your life and making it difficult for you to walk away.

5. **You Are Trauma-Bonded to Him**. These bonds are identical to Stockholm Syndrome. In this type of relationship, you are brainwashed into feeling loyalty toward him. And why does this happen? It is strictly because of the breaks in kindness that were extended to you to ease the pains that you are going through. And then you are forced to believe that every misdeed will always end with kindness. Therefore, the understanding that he gives temporarily will be confused with genuine care, and it will end up trapping you down waiting for the future that will not come.

6. **You've Been Gaslighted.** Narcissists will gaslight you, and you will start to question what's real about you. And then you stop to trust your intuition. You stop trusting your judgment, and you begin to feel if all your feelings are wrong. You begin to have difficulty understanding what is right about you. As a result, you trust his judgment and not yours. You see him ahead of you, and you don't see yourself as to be blamed. You prefer to stay in the relationship, thinking he's covering

up your mistakes and staying out will expose your lousy behavior.

7. **You Blame Yourself For The Problem in The Relationship.** When it comes to verbal and mental games of twisting and changing games, he is an expert. He makes the conversation where he knows he's wrong to be able to turn back at you. So often time your hearing of jealous, abusive, and name calling will keep occurring. But your mind will accept it to be an accident and not indeed the real occurrence.

8. **You feel Isolated From Support That Is Abundant For Your Pick.** Your Narcissist spouse may cut you off connections that might make you regain consciousness. Those friends that will question why you are still in the relationship, friends that will tell you that it's your fault for staying in the contact, people that will aid you to think critically. Regardless of what it is, you might feel like you do not have anyone who can be by your side which you will need to turn to in times of need, is it that you don't have? Not really. You are far from them, and that's your Narcissist's spouse antics.

9. **You Are Always Finding The Good in Him.** Truly, focusing on a person's fault all the time isn't healthy at all. But how long should you keep taking all the blame? How long

should you be taking all those insults? Instead of reasoning like that. You are convincing yourself that he's doing it unwillingly. You will believe that he has good intentions. You forgive easily and deep inside you wrestle with a devil that torment you every day thinking that one day, it will all be over.

10. **You Want The Relationship To End Formally**. See, it will never march in. Why? You already know. The narcissist doesn't want you to tell them you are cutting off, when you do, he comes angered and gets upset. That makes you think that he wants the relationship. He will step further and pleads that you stay. You have higher chances of staying as long as you have the intention of breaking up like a regular breakup. What works best is an unannounced breakup where you gradually distance yourself from him.

How to Deal With What You Passed Through

You've considered what you will feel why you are growing past the stage of healing, you've known why it is difficult to break free from a Narcissists relationship. But how do you finally take back your life? It takes time, and you don't expect this face to disappear within a short time. Because it involves your brain and body. They have to act their survival response.

They have to learn a new pattern and replace them with the old model that once existed.

And that critical concept that can help you to accomplish that is the ability to detach yourself emotionally. This is the process whereby you learn to understand what is yours and discard what is not yours and do so not out of fear but do it out of love for your life, and your consciousness.

You must be able to manage your inner thoughts, your body sensation, and your dreams. Doing this will allow you to grow and heal, leading to a tremendous transformation. Doing this is the only option that can guarantee that you have the right connection to yourself, you make an informed decision, and you can see the vision of a brighter future. Below are seven practical ways to take back your life and be who you want to be.

1. **Don't View The Narcissist From as Human.** This is not the time when you have to keep thinking about the narcissist. This is the time to start thinking about yourself, which is contrary to what a narcissist wants from you. They desire that you should get obsessed about trying to understand them and in the process, they bring in confusion-you have a distorted view about yourself and how you feel. At first, when

the thinking sets in, remind yourself that it is a trap and that your instinct was right for letting go. You can write down want you want in a relationship and tick them if you are getting in return any one of them, likely, you wouldn't be getting anyone back from them, and that tells you that your decision is right and just. So, feed on reality!

2. Let Go Of The Feelings to Let a Narcissist Get You. Now, this isn't a time where you should start explaining how the narcissist hurts you. Remember you've done that before you finally decided to reach this conclusion. It is pointless trying to get back on this again. When you keep explaining that, it feeds their desires, they have a sense of accomplishment. They see themselves as subverting you eventually. With that, you can hurt them by not finding the means to explain to them what you feel and why you wouldn't want to get to work a relationship with them again. When they call for an explanation, and you discontinue from telling them, you bruise their ego, and they get pained. Instead of making you think that what you have done is wrong, they get to ask themselves what tactics they played wrongly.

3. **Quickly Build a Circle Around You.** The more you stay thinking about what happened, the higher the chances of

feeling remorse, and getting an ugly treat. So to jump out of this situation, quickly move out of your comfort zone, find friends, if possible, drive long distances to look for an old friend who will reassure you of what true love is. Join a community program that focuses on how to heal from an abusive relationship. Also, if you have any desired game, call out friends to play together. It is essential that what you read matters a lot. Thus, read a book that mainly speaks on picking up your strength. You might decide to read on many books - that speaks or talks about the subject.

4. **Cut Off Contacts.** Don't forget that a narcissistic fellow will want to get back on you, they want to make you reconsider the relationship, the more you keep them within yourself, the more you can see them and interact with them once again. Therefore, if you have their contact, do away with it, if they are on any of your social networks, take them off. You aren't a sadist; you are just a realist!

But what if the relationship is with a co-worker. You will still be seeing them, and how can you do this, maintain a strict boundary. And be convinced that the limit you set is right. They may see it as being harsh, ignore it, you don't owe anyone - not even the narcissist, an explanation on how you live your life. If they are your parent, there is the likely hood that now that you are an adult you wouldn't need to stay with them, listen to them but insist on doing what you seem to feel right about.

5. **Demand For Balance**. And from who? Yourself! The chances are that you will feel imbalanced and the way you will regain your balance is by doing opposite what your narcissist does. Rather than feeding yourself with self-criticism that can emanate from how you've been dealt with, embrace self-knowledge. And often see the good in yourself. Slow down and focus well on improving the quality of your life. Push yourself beyond the comfort level. So always endeavor that you will desire to receive more. Drop the doubt; it is not part of you, that is not who you are. Once again write the negative thoughts you were thrown at while in the relationship, then in front of it, write the strength. Think about the qualities some people admire in you; get busy in developing those qualities. As you get busy building those qualities. You will pay less attention to the negative words that were said to you.

6. **Don't Try to Please Them**. It just goes in connection with the point discussed earlier. Although this is mostly

applicable if the narcissist is a co-worker. It can be applied with a person with an ex that you see just occasionally.

However, it doesn't mean that you can't do pleasing things for them when it is right for you to do that. The only caution is never to do it because you want to please them. Also, you don't want to expect expressing gratitude from them if you ever did a pleasing thing. If you expect recognition, you will hurt yourself the more because you will never get it. Before now, you already know that they feel that showing appreciation is only meant for weak souls and not for highly intellect humans like them.

Don't slave yourself in order to please them. And it will hurt you further if you think that you are going to win their favor. Oh! I'm even sure you must have outgrown this stage. And don't behave like them, be like a free person who finds delight in what he does every day.

7. **Help Others.** You might likely think that how does that add up since you also need help. But the reality is that helping others is another practical way to heal up from your condition. Take for example, do you know anyone who is trying to recover from the pain and the stabs from a Narcissist. Can you help them? Yes, you can be their friends, you can

convince them that they deserve the best and explain to them what the recovery stage might be like. Also, you must teach them that it is not right to dwell on them. Now, what will you accomplish by doing this?

The more you tell them, the more you are convinced too that you have made the right decision and getting back will never be a choice for you. There is more benefit apart from that. When you see that they are getting better, it convinces you that you are getting better too and you will get through finally. So, while you help them, you are also helping yourself in reaching an optimum level of conviction.

8. **Don't Pretend.** At times you have to feel that you aren't comfortable about the situation. Don't pretend that it doesn't happen; it hurts you the more when you do that. If the feelings come, admit it and formulate a plan that will make you discard the thought. Always be ready to feed positive with harmful at all times. It doesn't come better than that. A Narcissist might want to use these on you and would make you feel that you took a wrong decision.

But the more you realize that all these thoughts will come, then the more you are better in the position to combat the feeling accurately. Also, resist the urge to speak or discuss your feelings with the Narcissist. It's disastrous. Don't let him or her raise a topic of that subject. Keep to your principles, and don't let him judge you.

9. **Always Trust Yourself.** You may have been shamed, you may have been dammed or embarrassed for airing your opinion, and all these can have an influence on you. And that makes you want to feel more inclined with them. But the fact now is that you should learn to trust yourself. Don't entertain the thought of second-guessing yourself. And this might stop you from taken risk. But don't let that deter you.

Before you make a decision, always assure yourself that you will make the best decision. You can increase the result of your decision making by starting to do in-depth research before you make a decision. To avoid having a distorted view of yourself. You can even meet folks who know better than you and who wouldn't rub that on your face, instead, they will calmly take you by hands.

Then take responsibility for your actions, learning the act to take responsibility for your efforts will illuminate the difference between when it's your fault and when it is not your fault. The more you realize that the more you can trust yourself more about your decisions. Also, as you see that the choice you make heads toward success, this will encourage you more that you are out of the toxic relationship for good and nothing more than that.

10. **Find a Therapist**. The value of a therapist can't be overstressed. You can lead a life you so much desire with their help. A therapist will serve as both a counselor and a guide. They monitor your progress. They understand how you feel - they've handled several situations, and they know how you can pick your life up once again. Just ensure that you explain how you think - the odds and the goods so that they know where they are going to address.

With these ten practical ways to get back your life, I can assure you that you will be the person you need to be. Yes, you can get back to the best version of yourself.

How to Trust Yourself Again

You are aware that the feeling of being abused can leave you shattered and broken. And this can give you a hard time trusting people around you and your confidence.

It might go wrong that you will think that every person or potential person coming near you or trying to establish a relationship with you is a Narcissist. If you aren't careful, you will leave a lonely life that is derived from joy and good company.

But the glaring truth is that all that can change. As you read on, you will see how and what you can do to help the situation.

Well, after the Narcissist abuse, you might have difficulty making decisions even though minor. And then making a choice might be like a hard thing to do. And it will seem to you that your wishes are far off your reach. You keep doubting and doubting, and that becomes even closer to you than you think.

But could a memory down the lane help? How did it start?

While reading this book, you might have sensed that the problem emanated from gas lighting. A Narcissist placed you in a state of weakness. You will see something, but your Narcissist partner tells you no, and all your lines of defense seem as if there were all gone - wasted efforts.

Take for example, while watching a TV, you saw an object and you could see that the color is blue, you might be amazed that what you see is a green object a not blue; he will assure you that it is green, while he claims to have a better sight than you and he can solidly maintain that stand and position. He will go on by telling you that you misinterpreted the message or you had a wrong perception. And as he proceeds, you tend to start questioning your power of knowledge; you begin to question your instinct, you have been weakened, and you got so used to that that you have been designed for that particular abuse.

Frankly, though, those who are abusers emotional wouldn't do it intentionally. Is that surprising? They've been so ingrained in the attitude that they hate to see you in power or they hate to see you demand your joy and well-being and the way they set that it is through confusion and self-doubt.

And imagine going through this stage for not just one, not two or three years, some might have even been battling through this for more than a decade or two. Grooming yourself and not trusting yourself for that long time would have affected you that you will think it is the usual thing that could happen to a person. And at a point, you stop questioning.

In that stage, your health and just aggression have left you. You have agreed that you are cold not loving and having no affection for being angry at a wrong treatment received from the hands of Narcissist. Your reasons for an upset are right and just. You've gotten a boundary that has been shattered. You aren't oblivious to the fact that even though they claim to love you, they will still take from you what belongs to you at your own expense.

All you got is "it's your fault," and your balance is off the radar. And that makes you partially trust then and wonder if you are right.

And you know what all that has led to? Distrust! You can't trust yourself. It's the abuse and not that you don't have the ability to possess trust. What happened isn't your fault, instead is the Narcissists. But the harsh truth is that if you fail to get up, it will be your fault! And getting you to trust yourself and people around you again is a process that has to be handled kindly and gently.

Recovering The Trust You've Lost.

1. **Accepting The Abuse**. One of the fundamental recovery processes is acceptance. Believe that your partner possesses destructive traits, it has damaged your health, your mindset, and your self-esteem. Agreed that you were never loved the way you should have been loved. So, grieving that

person that abused you for a very long time is a first step to gain recovery.

Rage also happens to be a crucial step in aiding your revival. What you need to do, bring closer a note, pen down an exhaustive list of your partner's behavior. Write as many as possible. Label it: "Evil Traits." The more you see this, the more you can see the evil in the person, instead of hurting yourself, you continually see the evil and trust yourself for acting right all this while.

Also, reveal your vexation to the world, not turning to the madness style though, but speak out, this will convince you further that you were being used. You might likely even meet people who would say they knew all along, but we're scared to tell you. Also, you might be able to help someone not to fall into the prey of being used by a Narcissist too.

2. **Build a New Life.** I can't overemphasize the effect of building a new life around you. Start connecting to those who are ready to be your help in time of distress. As you go out in search of a modern lifestyle, write down the Traits you can accommodate in a relationship (I've spoken on what makes a good relationship), so you can use that as a guide.

3. **Reflect**. Yes, the better you understand what happened and why it happened, the higher the chances of not falling into the hands of the Narcissist. So, write down what happened, and the Traits the Narcissist portrays at the beginning of the relationship. This will function as a guide so you can watch for red spots and signs. And from afar, you can predict if you will be used and dumped at the end of the relationship or not.

CHAPTER FIVE

HELPING A NARCISSIST

Helping a Narcissist - If you Truly Love him

You might be willing to help your partner, who is a Narcissist. Although, it should be noted that you have to be careful and there is a point where you don't just want to hurt yourself trying to help. As a result of that, these are strategies that you might employ, which will help you to cope through quickly and you will be able to conclude that he doesn't need to be maintained.

1. **Check For Abuse.** No amount of suggestion to maintain a Narcissist will help if the individual tends to physically or emotionally abuse you. Although it is great to know that it is not all Narcissist that will turn abusive. But some do. Therefore, if you are facing abuse, don't ponder on

what's driven the abuse, abuse is abuse. And the abuser is fully responsible for the action. An abuser will always use you to their joy and happiness. They will often time feel no remorse for abusing you. Even if it is evident to you. The more you linger around thinking the time for help will come, it might be too late because you might lose your life in trying to wait for the right time to help an abuser.

If you sense these traits in the individual, do not try to render any help. It won't get better, it will only get worse, and any attempt to help might be damaging to your life.

2. **Check For Traces of Denial**. A lot of people today can sense denial as long as they see it. And that denial is the most mechanism used by Narcissist. For example, a person who indulges in alcohol and gets overboard would protest that he loves and enjoys the taste of wine and would not acknowledge that he is an alcoholic. Same can also be said of a person who is terminally ill; such an individual would say: oh! It's just a simple cough. So is a Narcissist who out of her attitude lost her job and friends, and later says: "I'm just doing pretty fine," all these are exhibiting denial, and it is obvious. The more a person expresses rejection, the more he is likely to accept help.

So, to give this help, be sure that your partner can admit to some wrongs. If it is little, watch sentences like "my life isn't where I thought it would be." Or I don't dream of having what is in front of me. All these are signals that the person needs help and would certainly get it if given more attention. I'm glad that some Narcissist has resulted in being helped; they have walked up to a therapist to improve their condition. But only the vulnerable ones will. They readily admit that they have problems instead of covering them up on the denial. And experiences have shown that they are more likely to stick with the treatment plan that they've been given by a therapist.

3. **Check For Manipulation**. Narcissist that have had a very high score on the level of exploitation and sense of entitlement has been said to have a very high degree of an impulse to cheat and to be aggressive. More to the point is the fact that when angered, they might result in stealing in return or sabotaging property at work. And then worst behavior that could be practiced comes from the end of a Narcissist.

Also, in levels of psychopathy and Machiavellianism, a Narcissist would have a higher score. They are both linked to callousness, criminal traits, and do whatever they feel like doing. Well, not all Narcissist will be cold and manipulative, but those who have the habit will have a very high degree of posing a threat because they've been practicing the art and deceit for a very long time to the point that you would have a hard time parting fact from fiction. Whatever they see as real is the truth and nothing else.

4. **Check Their Readiness to Change.** Although, this part might come so glaring for you to see. It has to be mentioned. And one way to test if a partner is willing to change his or her ways is to call on the help of a therapist. If they are ready and willing to work it out together with you and they didn't feel reluctant to seek advice from a therapist, it might be a clear sign that they will yield to treatment and are willing to change. That will also heighten the willingness to improve your relationship with that individual.

5. **Check For Your Silence.** Research points out that silent withdrawal has been a way to deal with feeling sad or fearful about our connection with people we love. And that might mean to go underneath the impulses to shut down and share the upset that exist. So, when you decide to keep calm about the situation and go so silent about it, your partner might be willing to hear your pain, and if they are so deep in their

Narcissistic behavior, then you know that resorting to silence wouldn't even push them to repent. Instead, they keep on.

So, watching your silence can be an excellent pointer to note where to draw the boundary. Coming down to you to hear from you might be a way to solidify a conversation that will lead him to agree to meet a therapist or rejecting the help a therapist will proffer.

6. **Be Honest With Yourself.** If you have tried and you've done all you could, but nothing comes beneficial. It might be that you've done all you could. It doesn't mean that you are a failure. It only suggests that the only hope that remains have been used.

But you have to be honest with yourself to be sure that you've really done all you could and that you have not substituted working so hard for feeding a sufficient amount of empathy.

After all, have been tried, the decision to stay in such a relationship lies in your hands. You have to admit either you are waiting because he's changing or it feels too hard to leave. But don't endure any hurt because you want someone to change.

But if you have verified and you discovered that they are ready to change. This subheading, the final one on this, will give you the treatment plans available.

Reliable Treatments For Narcissist Personality Disorder

If you've considered being of help to your Narcissist partner after carefully considering that they worth the support, or while reading this book, you've been convinced that you have this condition. Then, this part is going in-depth into the treatment plan that you will undergo - from therapies to what you should expect and - many more.

You'd recall that there isn't a cure to this condition, but there are treatment plans that can be given to patients which will be of help to their situation.

Most mental health conditions today are often treated with the combination of therapy and some use of medication. But when it comes to personality disorder which Narcissism is one of them, they don't respond to medication. So even if drugs are prescribed, they will only address the symptoms relating to co-occurring disorders that might present itself alongside the disorder.

People with Narcissist personality disorder are endeavor to undergo therapies that offer the most excelling possibilities of recovery. They include family, individual, and group therapy. When treatment is ongoing, and it is intensive, they are capable of addressing Narcissist personality disorder to halt the extent of damage that had been done to their life which has stopped them from reaching the potential they have to.

It is also noteworthy that the help provided by family members, friends, and other close associates might go a long way to give a boost to that realization.

When the treatment plan starts, therapists do not attack the situation aggressively or openly, and that is a chill of comfort. This is because Narcissism operates as a continual principle of personality. Therefore, the therapeutic process will undoubtedly include deliberate and careful approach so that that a patient isn't pushed either too far or too fast counteracting the primary motive of undergoing that help.

It is even noteworthy that both the therapist and the patient work together. This is done so that they can recognize the attitude and behavior that lead to stress, conflicts, and dissatisfaction in the patient's life. As the recovery progresses, the therapist often encourages the Narcissist to obtain constructive action so they can ameliorate the impact of their Narcissist symptoms. It doesn't stop there, and they go on to provide them with practical advice that can help them in accomplishing that.

Therapists that work with Narcissist patients must strive to create an atmosphere where the judgmental attitude is excluded, and that help is only based on solutions-oriented. This is so important since a positive approach in therapy can boost trust and lead to active dialogue between the doctor and patients.

As a result of that, there are several evidence-based therapy programs for patients diagnosed with Narcissist personality disorder.

Cognitive Behavioral Therapy. This entails multiple sessions of CBT. What patients accomplish here is to replace grandiose and distorted thoughts with more positive and realistic ideas and other self-assessments that are inclusive.

Psychodynamic Therapy. This form of therapy sessions with the patient and the therapist entails plumbing the depths of their previous experiences and will use that to validate the effects of problematic relationships in their lives and to examine any unconscious assumptions about themselves and others that support Narcissistic attitudes.

Family Therapy. Narcissistic behavior undeniably impacts individuals, and it changes the family too. Also, the healing and recovery process involves family members, as well. This is to help family members understand the real motive behind Narcissist self-centered behavior.

Generally, it has been seen that Narcissist patients at the early stage of their therapies, they are often resistant, and that is why mental health professionals often strive to work overtime, so they ensure their patients are entirely doing fine with all the treatment plans that are being given to them. So naturally a Narcissist does not expect full cooperation at the initial stage, but as the treatment plan goes on, the Narcissist keeps learning what to do so that they can be confident of recovering finally.

Nevertheless, while outpatient therapy can be efficient for a long-term option, Narcissist who are new to recovery should be taken to a residential mental health facility. That way, an inpatient recovery program is designed for such individual so that they can get intense and therapeutic experience. In that way, counselors are available regularly to help provide customized treatment services and continuous encouragement and other support that can be granted morally.

Narcissist patients who are being attended to in residential facilities are also able to obtain intensive treatment for the symptoms of any co-occurring emotional or behavioral health conditions that might be available, which isn't to be taken lightly — the rate of substance use disorders, anxiety disorders, and other mood disorder.

When there is a development of co-occurring conditions, people who are suffering from them need a very comprehensive and integrated treatment service that will focus on targeting their Narcissistic traits and several other mental health issues simultaneously and in a more fully coordinated manner. Also, residential treatment is often followed if there are severe symptoms of the co-occurring disorder and are also efficient for those undergoing harsh health conditions.

Although many claim that recovery programs dedicated to those who are Narcissist are low, but with an inpatient treatment plan, it offers a very speedy result. Since they are distracted with unstable home life, requirements at school, children need, many questions from family members about their recovery process.

Furthermore, residential treatment centers have been able to significantly assist a lot

of people with a personality disorder to get over distorted and self-destructive patterns of thinking and behavior. They presented tremendous hope for those with this condition and have eventually found courage in admitting that they have a problem that can't be solved on their own.

Long Term Recovery From Narcissistic Personality Disorder.

Narcissists often deny the depth and the nature of their problems even after they've resolved to seek for help.

But as soon as that initial resistance is over, they begin to listen to their therapists and then starts to reflect on the consequences that their attitude brings, which will now result into a positive outcome that will be anticipated.

So, once they agree that they have a deep problem - not that they don't have a problem this time, they will be able to analyze themselves critically. And frankly, this is an essential aspect of enabling them to step forward so they can address their past and then focus more on the future - a better one. This will create a better way of thinking.

So, without treatment, a Narcissist will not change or get better. No wonder Narcissists who have presented themselves for treatment have gotten and adopted a very high degree of improvement. They admitted their true feelings and have also been able to clarify and enlighten themselves.

Alongside these treatment plans, there are a lifestyle and home remedies that should be taken into consideration. These are discuses below.

Life Style And Home Remedies.

Even before you go to a therapist and during the treatment plan, you have to consider these lifestyle and home remedies. This is because initially your narcissist partner or if you are with the condition might feel defensive and think that the therapy isn't worth your time and money thus wanting to quit. But, do the following if you think that way.

1. **Keep an Open Mind.** Yes, you need to focus on the rewards of treatment. Just don't be distracted with whatever thinking comes to your mind. If you have a thought that is aimed at distracting you, always remind yourself that the effort will genuinely pay- your family, friends, and partners want the best in you.

2. **Stick to Your Plan.** Always attend to your schedule sessions and take necessary medication that is given to you. Although, it can be hard work and there might be an occasional setback, but you will undoubtedly win through. You might ask a friend to keep track of the time you need to take specific medication, set a reminder to continually remind you when you need to go for a visit or use a drug.

3. **Be Treated For Other Conditions.** Alcohol abuse, misuse of drugs, and other mental condition like depression and anxiety can lead to stress, which will make you have pain emotionally and develop emotional behavior. Therefore, speak up with your health professional about the need to get this treatment. The earlier he or she knows, the better

4. Remain Focused. Always stay motivated and keep reminding yourself of the goals you have. No better joy comes from planning a goal and reaching it. It gives you more personal contentment, and you have more happiness that you can achieve whatever is set before you.

While preparing for your appointment, there are things to be done, which will also enhance the outcome of the results that you have.

ss1. **List Any Symptoms You Are Experiencing And The Length.** This will assist your health care provider in determining the type of events that are likely to trigger your anger or upsets you.

2. **List Out Personal Information.** Endeavor to include traumatic events that have happened to you in the past and any current major stressor that you are battling with.

3. **Write Down Medication information-** Do not forget to list any physical or mental health conditions that you have been diagnosed to be battling with.

4. **Write Down Medications.** Either herbs, supplements, or other vitamins, do not forget to write them down. It helps

the doctor to know which treatment plan will be of immense help to you.

Don't forget to write down questions that you will need your doctor to answer. It is very, very important.

When going, do not forget to go along with a family member or friend. Going with you will assist you in remembering some minor or little details. Also, in the process of inquiry from you, a person who has known you for a very long time could assist in asking you some basic questions and then render assistance in sharing valuable information with you.

Regardless, below are important questions that need to be asked by you. These questions are expected to be answered by your medical health practitioner.

- What kind of disorder do you think I'm battling with?

- Is it possible that I have other mental health condition?

- What is the goal of the treatment that you will be prescribing for me?

- What treatment plans are most likely to be very useful for me?

- How much degree or extent do you think my quality of life could improve to?

- How regular will I need therapy sessions and for how long?

- Should I consider family, individual, or group therapy?

- Are there medications that can be used to reduce my symptoms?

- I have some other health conditions. In what best ways can I manage them with this?

- Do you have any brochure or printed publication that I can be referred to?

- Are there websites you recommend that I visit and read from?

If you have any question apart from these, do not feel reluctant to ask.

However, below, you can find some of the things you can expect from your mental health provider. He or she may ask you:

- What are your symptoms?

- When do these symptoms start to occur and how long do they last?

- How do those symptoms affect the quality of your life, including work, personal relationship, and even school?

- How do you feel and act if you are being criticized or rejected?

- Is there any close personal relationship that you presently have? If you don't, why do you think you aren't in any?

- Do you have a significant accomplishment?

- Do you have goals for the future, what are they?

- When your help is needed, how do you feel?

- When painful feelings are being expressed, how do you feel? Emotions like sadness and fear?

- How would you describe your childhood and your relationship with your parents?

- Do you have any close relatives that have been diagnosed with a mental health disorder like a personality disorder?

- Have you ever been treated for any mental health problems, if so, which of the treatments is the most effective?

- Do you use alcohol or have you ever indulged yourself in drugs, if so, how often?

- Are you currently undergoing any current medical condition?

All these are what you should bear in mind in your treatment plan either for yourself and that of your partner. One thing is evident if therapies are followed up correctly, with keen concern to instruction and with a positive mindset, a Narcissist can change for the better.

CONCLUSION

Whether you have been dealing with a Narcissist for a long time, or from self-examination, you've concluded that you are one, or this is your first time of getting comprehensive understanding of what Narcissism is all about, you will agree with me that experiences with a Narcissist can leave one traumatized, and if one is not careful, the trauma will last for the rest of one's life. And for that reason, getting a glimpse into how it works is fundamentally vital to either avoid the situation, better manage the situation or render help to those who likely need to be helped so they can manage their condition better.

As a recap, this book has extensively given concise understanding of who a Narcissist is, it has explained how they are made, and it didn't fail to highlight some of the backgrounds. Also, the book has comprehensively showed that Narcissism, even though it can't be cured, it can be treated and managed. So, you aren't a novice to what Narcissism is all about. But that itself isn't enough.

Therefore, you read further on the types that exists- the exhibitionists, the covert, and the toxic ones. You've been able to see the similarities that exist between them and the differences. You can better tell if a person is either a toxic Narcissist or a closet. And this knowledge led the way to understand how to avoid them.

In explaining how to avoid and deal with them. I started by analyzing the techniques they use and how they carry out those techniques, you've been able to examine your relationship and see whether you are in a relationship with a Narcissist and how you can help the situation. And finally, this book analyzed how you can deal with them without resorting to anger and aggression, so you don't worsen the situation.

The fourth chapter has helped you see how the healing process works. You have been able to see what a person who has been dealt with by a narcissist will undergo, why most people find it difficult to let go, how to deal with what you have passed through, and how you can regain trust again.

The final part has thoroughly explained what you should expect in a treatment plan, and all that has to be taken into proper consideration before you head to the therapist and while you there. Now with all these, what can be concluded?

First, if you have validated that you are a Narcissist, it is highly reasonable and helpful that you seek medical care and start with a diagnosis of your condition. Secondly, if you have a family member that is having these traits but has not to lead to physical abuse, you can ask him, or her to read from this awesome book. After reading, the two of you can visit a doctor for proper validation. And that way proper diagnosing and thorough investigations will be made.

Finally, be assured that a life that is free from the hands of a Narcissist promises tranquility, good health, and can add quality to ones living. Life is worth living when we are surrounded with people who think more of others than themselves. These ones are willing to help at all times.

While narcissism doesn't have include good traits, learning on how to cultivate good traits will go a long way to make the world a better place for everyone. You should use the knowledge you have gained from reading this book to guide you in every decision you make. Always think of the pains and the trauma people will undergo if they are not dealt with accordingly. Be motivated always to act rightly and kindly!